Everything
Donald Trump
Knows About
Leadership

Making Books Great Again

by We The People

DEDICATION

To the extensive team of researchers who worked tirelessly to assemble everything that Donald Trump knows about this subject.

ABOUT THE AUTHOR

We The People began writing on January 20, 2017 when the United States was temporarily seized by a delusional, cabbage-smelling tyrant with tiny hands that dwarfed his IQ. We The People will continue producing work that exposes the vastlessness of his knowledge until the country is reclaimed.